Family

La familia

lah fah-*meel*-yah

Illustrated by Clare Beaton

Ilustraciones de Clare Beaton

mother
mom

la madre

lah *mah*-dreh

la mamá

lah mah-*mah*

father
daddy

el padre

ehl *pah*-dreh

el papá

ehl pah-*pah*

parents

los padres

lohs *pah*-drehs

sister

la hermana

lah ehr-*mah*-nah

brother

el hermano

ehl ehr-*mah*-noh

uncle

el tío

ehl *tee*-oh

aunt

la tía

lah *tee*-ah

cousins

los primos

lohs *pree*-mohs

grandmother
grandma

la abuela

lah ah-*bweh*-lah

la abuelita

lah ah-bweh-*lee*-tah

grandfather
grandpa

el abuelo

ehl ah-*bweh*-loh

el abuelito

ehl ah-bweh-*lee*-toh

grandparents

los abuelos

lohs ah-*bweh*-lohs

A simple guide to pronouncing Spanish words

- Read this guide as naturally as possible, as if it were English.
- Put stress on the letters in *italics*, for example, *lee* in ah-bweh-*lee*-tah.

La familia	lah fah-*meel*-yah	**Family**
la madre	lah *mah*-dreh	**mother**
la mamá	lah mah-*mah*	**mom**
el padre	ehl *pah*-dreh	**father**
el papá	ehl pah-*pah*	**daddy**
los padres	lohs *pah*-drehs	**parents**
la hermana	lah ehr-*mah*-nah	**sister**
el hermano	ehl ehr-*mah*-noh	**brother**
el tío	ehl *tee*-oh	**uncle**
la tía	lah *tee*-ah	**aunt**
los primos	lohs *pree*-mohs	**cousins**
la abuela	lah ah-*bweh*-lah	**grandmother**
la abuelita	lah ah-bweh-*lee*-tah	**grandma**
el abuelo	ehl ah-*bweh*-loh	**grandfather**
el abuelito	ehl ah-bweh-*lee*-toh	**grandpa**
los abuelos	lohs ah-*bweh*-lohs	**grandparents**

© Copyright 1994 B SMALL PUBLISHING, Surrey, England.

First edition for the United States, Canada, and the Philippines published 1996 by Barron's Educational Series, Inc.

All rights reserved. No part of this book may be reproduced in any form, by photostat, microfilm, xerography, or any other means, or incorporated into any information retrieval system, electronic or mechanical, without the written permission of the copyright owner.

Address all inquiries to: Barron's Educational Series, Inc., 250 Wireless Boulevard, Hauppauge, New York 11788.

ISBN-13: 978-0-7641-0042-0

ISBN-10: 0-7641-0042-4

Library of Congress Catalog Card Number 96-85809

Printed in China   19 18 17 16